Anentropy

- an expression of love in poetry and prose

Lance Reid

Published/Produced by Anentropy, LLC

Anentropy, LLC

Crestview Hills, KY

Anentropy

ISBN 978-0-9823855-4-8

Dedicated to Stefanie, my inspiration for this book, my wife.

Contents

My Turf

New Order

The Hunter

Love

Thumbnail

Inspiration

Honorable Chameleon

*When All the World Does Fall at
Beauty's Feet*

*What Torturous Wounds a Hundred
Days Hath Wrought*

*The Clock Does Move, but Slowly
Toward My Time*

*"What Move Would Make Her
Happy?" is My Thought*

One Moment

Explanation

I wrote this book for my bride-to-be twenty years ago. Now, as we approach our twentieth anniversary, we enjoy a healthy, full life. We have three wonderful kids who keep us on our toes, and a strong sense of family, church, and community.

With the twentieth anniversary approaching, people have been asking me what it takes to be married for twenty years, seemingly headed for fifty and more. And while the long answer includes examples of work, dedication, compromise, forgiveness, giving, and more, the simple answer is that all these things are reflections of one thing - love. Puppy love is fun. Honeymoon love is pretty sweet. But the type of love requires dedication and effort is the love with the greatest payout.

This book is the best way I have to express that love. It is a combination of poetry and prose. It is a bearing of the soul. And since love is not an emotion exclusive to me, you will also find elements of your love as you read.

Girls - if this book is a gift from your husband or husband-to-be, know that he picked it because he found elements of his love in here as well. His interpretation may be different than yours, and he may not relate to everything in here. That's not the point, and trying to extract his interpretation may be a very painful process for both of you. The point is that he thought, "This might do a good job of expressing my love, since I'm a guy and don't do a very good job of that."

Guys - if this book is a gift from your wife or wife-to-be, know that she saw something in here and thought, "That's us!" After you read through it, ask her what part made her think that. Reread it if needed. Comment on how it is like you, or find out why she thinks so.

That's enough of my relationship advice! Enjoy the book.

Prologue

I love you madly. This book is part of my wedding gift to you, and it is intended to say just that - "I love you madly." This prologue is the last thing being written, and is being completed just one month before the ceremony, but what is hard to see is the work that has been going on over the past seven months.

You see, for nearly a year now, I've been watching all the work you have put into the wedding. True, I've worked on the honeymoon, stuffed invitations, and helped in other ways when I can, but you have obviously put in tons of work for the wedding. I can see your love for me in the work you are doing.

That's why, around May, when I thought about our married life, I realized that having the pictures and videos and memories of the wedding would be a permanent reminder of the love you have for me. I thought it would be nice to have some sort of permanent reminder that would symbolize the love I have for you. More so than beautiful jewelry, but something that required time, effort, concentration, and organization - a long term project similar to planning a wedding.

So I began writing the poetry and the text, compiling a book to serve as a reminder of my love for you. So this gift is the result. While it may not be on the same level as planning a large wedding, it was a significant effort born out of love. I hope you like it. Of course, the jewelry is also a symbol of my love, and a good backup plan in case this book flops!

Not only are all these poems written just for you, but none of them have ever been read by any other person. Perhaps we'll share them sometime, but these are all written specifically for you, and the content of each poem has been kept secret. While I have described the gift, and requests have been made to see a sample, I have denied those requests, wanting your eyes to be the first to see them.

So I hope the guy binding the book doesn't read them!

Each poem is surrounded by text, and so the first poem follows. This is the only "previously released" poem. While I'm not sure if anyone besides you ever read it, this poem was written specifically for you when you underwent sleep deprivation testing, and is meant to capture that feeling of an overpowering tiredness. I never showed it to anyone else, but you may have. Nevertheless, it was written just for you, so it is included.

I hope you enjoy all this. I know you worked hard on the wedding, and I am quite impressed.

I love you madly.

Dreamtime

Forced

She shudders

Down nature path.

Dance softly in the clearing, Halluce and Life

On wingless foot, float from the light,

One within, share audience tonight.

Forbidden fruit

Twists wild in wind.

Patterns shake 'til

Trickling dust, remains unseen

'Til all the world whirls 'round the scene

And rolls away to other dreams.

Left.

Alone.

Stand in the clear.

Sail ship whips in

To pick a steer.

Board quickly now, as sea does form
And steer the sleeping back to norm
Who twist to roll another storm.

So the title of this book is Anentropy. I feel it is only appropriate that I spend some time defining that title, especially if I am to say, and I am saying, that anentropy defines our marriage. I do not know if the word anentropy exists. We have already established the fact that I can not have an original thought, so I am sure that the word exists. But please refer to any definitions expressed or implied in this book. If the word really does exist, I'm sure I've missed the mark of its true meaning.

Scientifically speaking, entropy defines the disorder in the universe. Entropy is based on the idea that everything in the universe is moving toward a state of disorder. This is evident by the suggestion that Rick Pitino may leave the University of Kentucky.

I should point out, in case this personal novel ever becomes public, that Rick Pitino is a genius. The University of Kentucky can survive without him, but glory is inevitable while Pitino is there. I hope he stays. As long as he never coaches at the University of Louisville, the world will keep spinning.

There is another subject in science, or engineering, or pop culture, that is called chaos.

Chaos shows up as an unpredictable "disturbance" in experiments. It is a kind of interference or random variance whose cause can not be found. It has been suggested that this chaos actually has order. Furthermore, it is suggested that if we knew the original state, we could predict the future. A meteorologist suggested this idea.

Incidentally, chaos can not be the scapegoat for abnormally large disturbances in my electrical experiments. The university installed a large electrical ground beneath the building to eliminate electrical disturbances. Unfortunately, when the building was erected, as if I use such words, they forgot to connect the building to the electrical ground. That's why my experiments were so unstable. I believe that problem has since been addressed.

It is my theory that this chaos, an apparently random disturbance, but one that has distinct patterns, is a kind of measure of entropy. "Poem Chaos" serves as an example of this chaos. It is apparently random babble generated by a healthy mix of 4-year-old Jim Beam and Mountain Dew, but is actually a mix of pairs of lines. That is to say, each line has a mate.   So, it's more of an entertaining puzzle than a poem.

Chaos

My favorite beer costs $2 per bottle.

Alliance for mentally ill blames Hollywood for discrimination.

Bruce Lee played Kato in The Green Hornet.

Elvis only paid Priscilla $1000 per month in alimony.

Animal rights activists attack fur wearers.

Johnny Carson's ex-wives get tons of $'s.

A mentally ill man attacked lions at the Bronx Zoo.

Bill Clinton champions allowing gay people to serve in the military.

There's only 1 Bullet Train in the US.

9 our of 10 employers seek leadership.

The Village People liked the Navy.

Government allows companies to dump waste in the ocean.

I've got a lifelong pass on a Bullet Train.

The Green Hornet's name was Bret Reid (almost).

I can't put clear and brown glass in the same recycling bin.

Possums in New Zealand are overpopulated due to declining fur sales.

Your employer is a 1 out of 10 company.

I drink a beer that costs 42 cents per can.

The chaos is an unpredictable reaction, while entropy is a measure of unpredictability. As mentioned, entropy is based on the idea that everything in this universe is moving toward disorder. It is not too difficult to imagine the creation of something from nothing as a kind of expansion in God's hands. Likewise, one can picture that same creation in a compression stage, with the hands pushing closer together.

Thus I propose that just as we can see things moving toward disorder, and all processes result in excess heat, and this universe is expanding - I propose that the universe could also shrink, everything moving towards order, and all processes resulting in excess cool.

This heat and cooling thing has been in my mind since before high school. It was my theory that we have accidentally created cooling devices (refrigerators, air conditioners, etc.) that only cool by producing more heat. That is why you can not cool your kitchen by opening the refrigerator. I planned on developing a cooling device that did not produce more heat.

I now propose that such a process can only happen in a shrinking universe, or in an shrinking portion of a universe. In that proposal is my second proposal, which is that portions of a universe can be expanding while others are contracting, or being compressed. My next theory is that we can create an shrinking area in an expanding universe.

I have no idea how.

But when it is done, I hope that some young archaeologist, digging through the ruins of a shrinking universe, finds this print of a genius, centuries ahead of his time, who predicted the ability to control entropy.

And ordinary men can dream.

But enough science. The point is that I have a name for this state of compression, this wonderful pocket of a universe where everything is moving toward order: anentropy. I have only one real life example, which is the topic of the poem "Anentropy." You'll see the poem is not about science, but the concept of things coming together in a world that is drifting farther and farther apart.

Anentropy

Violence Spinning.
Control relinquished.
Apparent Chaos is
Anything but.
A world of entropy
Spinning, twisting,
Turning away
As the proponents
of decay
Fight to resist that
of which they are made.
Like the fiery waters bearing down,
An unstoppable force of nature renowned.

Yet this apparent entropy
Provides the current of the stream
As two salmon start their life's journey
Toward happiness, it's you and me
Thus we define anentropy.

Now, if we are not yet lost in the babble, I would like to give a brief example of how we are moving toward order. Keep in mind that we are back into one of those my time/your time things. I am writing this before we are married. Actually I am writing this in mid-May, 1993. I do not know what day it is without moving across the room to look at my Far Side calendar. Suffice it to say that I bought all the plane tickets for our trips between June and August on this day, in order to save big bucks before the prices go up at Continental Airlines.

Anyway, that's in my time. In your time, it is after our marriage. Who knows when. If we are scared to have, you know, sex, you may be reading this on our wedding night. Maybe we are flying over the Pacific, toward beautiful Australia. Or maybe our life in Jersey has begun. I enjoy picturing when you will read each poem. Anyway, whenever it is, it is now your time.

Incidentally, a third time "zone" could be considered for the young archaeologist finding this text. She or he will most likely be really confused about this whole discussion, so there is no need for embellishment of the third time zone.

Back to the moving toward order thing. All the time we are spending apart is being spent in an effort to move together. Our whole lives can be spent moving closer together. But that doesn't mean that this time apart isn't difficult. I am fully aware of this, believe me.

In that light, the poem "Home" focuses on our time apart, and our coming together. By the way, the mention of Cleopas, taken from the Bible, Luke 24, comes after two nearly consecutive sermons on the subject. On Easter, April 11, Larry, at my Methodist church, preached on the walk to Emmaus. On April 25, the day I became Catholic, you and I listened to a sermon on the same topic. That was special to me. I mentioned the coincidence, but not the significance. It exemplified the notion that I was not making such a significant transition.

Home

Brief encounter
Over Quickly
always left you feeling blue.

Slipped so briefly
through time's fingers
On the breeze away it flew.

Sitting quietly
Waiting wildly
For it all to start anew.

Just like Cleopas
and his friend
Only with them 'til they knew.

Try to pin it
To a schedule
Going to try it every two.

But when schedule
Crosses schedule
We just had to miss a few.

But keep holding
Grasping tightly
For you know that if you do,

I'll come home
To give my all
I've come home to marry you.

One of the aspects of my sense of humor is that I like to make fun of things that other people take seriously. For example, and this is common with other people as well, I will make overt, obnoxious, male chauvinistic comments. When in intelligent company, like you, or others who make fun of such an attitude, it is obviously a joke about men who really think that way. I make fun of my fancy new clothes, because I think it's silly to put a lot of weight in the brand name of my clothing.

But there's no sense in trying to convince anyone that I am joking about such things, because nobody believes me anyway. After all, they take it seriously. So perhaps I am just entertaining myself. I'm okay with that.

Another thing I joke about is my body, and my new muscles and such which are a result of an interest in Tai Chi. While some of my comments are made in jest, I freely admit that I am happy being more "fit."

Everyone knows that uplifting feeling you have after being on a workout program for a while. That energy you feel during the day. Call it high metabolism, call it the Chi, call it power, we've all felt strong and energetic.

For some strange and twisted reason, when I am feeling that way and am walking down the halls of my work, I feel the urge to jump up. High school boys do this sort of thing all the time, jumping to touch a door frame or a basketball rim or something like that. Not to be sexist or anything. High school girls may have had the same urges, but few ever acted on them. Besides, I proved to be the last person to know what was going on inside a high school girl's head.

Anyway, I think that is all I am wanting to do, to jump up and hit the exit sign, or the elevator numbers, or the ceiling. I have wondered what it would be like to be able to jump up into the rafters above the ceiling, pulling myself away from the hallway, and into a new and exciting world above the hallway, like a playground a child finds high in the trees.

And that is the subject of this next poem, jumping through the hallway ceiling tiles. The jump itself is the exciting part, not the experience of being up there. It would be kind of a disappointment to get up there and realize that I was still just me, an average employee who just destroyed a $20 ceiling tile and possibly burned his hand on a hot water pipe or something.

Ceiling Tile

Quietly, discretely,
Walking down the hall
As thousands of others do daily.

Attentions are focused elsewhere
If anywhere, as I walk down the hall,
But all present are aware of me.

Calm-like and peaceful,
Nothing to disturb
The soothing grind of the daily routine.

Suddenly, cleanly,
In an instant I move
Leap toward the ceiling to exit the scene.

A bold flash, a burst,
A disturbance of sorts,
One hand thrusts tiles aside
Other grasps metal

Lifting body through sliver.
Pulling up and then twist to fit
In with the rafters.

The others do notice
But forget again quickly
As order returns and quiet again rules

Quietly, discretely
Disappeared from them all
As thousands of others do daily.

OK, so I just added the part about people disappearing from the scene and being quickly forgotten. That may be interpreted as us leaving town after the wedding, and seems a bit sad that we might be forgotten. For some shallow people (no names, but you can think of a couple), it may be true, which may be all for the better. But good friends will remember and be in touch until our joyful return.

Speaking of joyful returns, it's always fun to return to Kentucky and find you waiting there. When I am sitting on the plane, it's as if I have something I want to share with everyone. Usually, I just sit there. Occasionally, though, I get to tell someone my story, and sometimes I hear a good story, get to know the kids, etc. One guy and I talked for quite some time after I helped to show his daughter where her mother was sitting on the plane (I had the aisle seat). Yet other times, you have to be careful, because there are some people who you just don't want to get started.

Anyway, I'm getting off track. You're probably wondering what "on track" is about now. Well, maybe it's time I explained the book some more:

Poems are spontaneous. They're either there or they're not. I am a huge believer in the creative mood. My poems, and other ideas, seem to come in clusters.

And you can't really guide the subject of a poem to any great extent. You can guide the words after you get the idea, usually, but sometimes you can't even do that. The really wild ones, where the words just kind of show up on the page, are my favorites to go back and read. I can just feel the excitement.

So after I get some poems, I add some text in between to guide the thoughts from place to place, and to break up the monotony. Kind of like the cheese and crackers at a wine tasting.

Anyway, the transition here was less than smooth. And that's... OK. But this next poem sort of comes together at the end, with the best sentiment and the best rhythm of the verse. That is an intentional effect.

Who, What, When, Where, Why

Sitting at the American Airlines terminal
Wonder why
The agent speaks in Spanish?
Aren't we in America?
Aren't we all American?
Are we not cohesive anymore?

Flying high 'cross friendly skies
Knowing where
My destination lies
Cincinnati? Northern Kentucky?
Either will be just as nice
If I see her when I arrive.

Kiss and Hug, we're on our way
Who knows what
We'll do today
Off to shop for wedding gifts?
Off to see our long lost friends?
We could use another day.

Before too long, I'm on my send
Ready when
The madness ends
To wake together every day
And kiss our morning breath away
Or brush our teeth and try it then.

The last of wondering left to do
Is over who
Will do this too?
She, of course, accepts the ring
We can share in every thing
Let rice be thrown, and angels sing.

Actually, that last one was written at the American Airlines terminal, where, across the hall, the immigration office was deporting a lot of people to the Dominican Republic. Kind of ironic that American Air was going to carry them out of the country!

But in the true spirit of the creative mood, another poem struck me as we were taxiing to the runway, based on a childhood experience you've heard about before. That poem follows.

Incidentally, the "whirlwind" part of the poem was written as we accelerated down the runway, and is quite illegible on paper. It was quite exhilarating to write it that way.

The childhood story, which you will now hear again, is about Chris, a guy who is 3 or so years younger than me, and whose Mom was good friends with my Mom. I feel Mom should always be capitalized, as should Dad, whether it is being used as a name or not. Don't hold me to this, though, as I may at times forget to capitalize, falling back on proper English instead.

Anyway, Chris was always pretty fun to play with, for a little kid - ha, ha. Seriously, he was cool. But when it would come time to leave, he would mysteriously misplace his shoes. His

Mom would yell at him to get his shoes, and he would yell and cry that he didn't want to leave and that he couldn't find his shoes. I guess I was a pretty good host.

Anyway, my Mom was cool about it. I'm sure she knew that I knew where the shoes were, but she never tried to force me into snitching on Chris. Maybe we should let Mom read this part, she's always wondering if I have any happy childhood memories, and she says fighting with my brother doesn't count. Nonetheless, the shoes are the topic here.

The Final Visit

The trip starts quickly, rushing 'round
To make the most of time in town
And then find time to settle down
But thoughts of leaving bring a frown.

Always fun, the time we spend
Even boredom's heaven sent
The time goes quickly by, and then
I'm carried off upon the wind.

But this time when it's time to go
I'll put my foot down, screaming "NO!"
I just won't go
I'm firmly lodged
Never to be moved again
Shaken, taken
from this spot
on which I stand
A rock, a fortress

Here to stay,
forevermore
'Til death
I say.

Childlike, then, my smile anews
"We can't leave now... I hid my shoes!"

Another mark of time: tonight is August 4. I have several more poems written, so I'm catching up on commentaries. Tonight I suggested that after we get married, we hide our shoes, so that we can't leave. I think it's a great idea. You were not as impressed, but maybe I'll be able to change your mind. Maybe if we shared it on our 50th wedding anniversary or something . . .

Anyway, that may just be one of those things you want to ignore and maybe I'll forget about it by the time we get married. Another thing you may have already forgotten about is the urge I have to jump into the ceiling in my halls at work. Wilson, the neighbor who knows it all on the TV show Home Improvement, may suggest that this is a primitive feeling that relates to man's urge to return to the trees, swinging from the vines.

To Wilson's point, we used to swing on the vines in the woods behind our house. To get to our mighty fortress, you had to either swing on a vine or walk the 2x4s across the creek. Actually, you could kind of step over the creek, but that wasn't any fun.

Did I say something about the prose between poems serving as an effective transition from one poem to the next? I may have to take that back sometime here, if I can't prevent rambling. My point about all the woods and such was that, possibly, that is the same feeling I have when I think about penetrating the ceiling tiles in the office building.

Anyway, the reappearing character in this book has finally decided to jump through the ceiling. The initial burst may have been just as exciting as imagined, but after that comes the problem of being up in the ceiling. What happens next?

Now I'm There

I've done it now
I've made the leap
I'm in the rafters
Just to see
What kind of nonsense down below
Is caused now by my lack of show
And tell me that they'll be amazed
And walk around for days and dazed
Out of their minds, where could he be?
He's gone two hours, maybe three

More beers will make this all come true
Or lots of Beam and Mountain Dew.

But what's this now, there's nothing said.
I could be gone and left for dead.
One came looking, heard him groan
"He's never here. I should have known."
The only notice of the day
Came from my brand new office mate

Who, as he left here for the night
Paused briefly to turn off my light.

Tomorrow is another day
They'll notice surely in some way
I guess for now I'll have to stay.

Quite a strange character, this rafter monkey. Incidentally, should anyone be relating to this poem, and the urge to live in the rafters, the ideal job may be a gaffer for a movie set. If you watch the movie credits to any movie, which I guess I am admitting to having done from time to time, you will notice someone who has the title "Gaffer." This is someone who climbs into the rafters in the morning and doesn't come down until night. Presumably they take care of lights and stuff like that. I think the ultimate goal is to become "Key Gaffer." Something to shoot for. Something for which to shoot.

Not that anything is wrong with watching the credits. How else would I know that the characters in "The Princess Bride" were all fitted with colored contacts so they would have blue eyes? All except for Prince Humperdinck and Tyrone, of course, because they are evil. Also, Monty Python likes to screw around with the credits, so you really have to pay attention.

Funny how that earlier comment about some archaeologist finding this book and deciding that it was written by a genius has kind of been shattered, huh?

Maybe the rafters would be a good place for me. It certainly would provide a new perspective on things (get ready for a really smooth transition). Every now and then the rut catches up with you. Even the last few poems, although refined and shaped just as I want them to be, even these have started to fall into a certain pattern. This is not something I wanted to do. Once in a rut, the book would quickly become repetitious, simply saying the same thing over and over. Redundant.

So I made a conscious attempt to break free from any mold. It took a couple tries. This first attempt has that charming quality of a car that won't start, but for some reason I liked it, so I included it.

Actually, I haven't thrown out any poems, but I have done major revisions on a few. So the fact that I kept this one is rather insignificant. It's still catchy, though, in a way.

Creative Sputter

Bust out of rhythm
Shake the shackles from your heart
Breath the air
Free to meander the earth
In nonsensical jubilation of the joy one finds
In knowing that love exists
Outside the confines of the structure.

Run with naked soul
Toward the sun's eternal light
Until, exhausted, you fall to the ground
And rest in its warmth.

Spin, and watch the world go by
The fields, the brook
As we alight on heaven's wings
Soaring beyond ceiling tiles, rooftops

Basketball courts, Pittsburgh,

Cincinnati, New Jersey, Daytona, all beneath
our sights

Feast our eyes on sights unseen

And we'll all rest a little easier tonight.

See what I mean? It would start to go on its own, but then fall back into a tractable rhythm. Tractable is a word, by the way, it has to do with Information Theory. I clarify that in case a particular Honor's English teacher ever reads this. She would say that tractable is not a word, so I should get a goose egg for a grade. But it is an Engineering word. Ergo, I can use it. I would also like to point out that I don't underline the word "ergo." I see no need in overemphasizing the fact that the word is Latin, and I take the grade deduction.

Speaking of that class, what kind of a person assigns attendance to a feminist rally as a homework assignment for the study of ancient literature? And on the same night as a major basketball game? Needless to say, even though I fully support equality, I got a zero on that assignment. She also changed it from "optional" to "mandatory" after she found out I didn't attend. Good times. But enough about her.

Not only do I support equality, but I also support quotas. Let me clarify that: I would prefer not having to take extraordinary efforts to vet out minority candidates, but I understand that without doing so, certain people would never change. So it is necessary.

For example, when a team on which I served was told to select the new Dean of Engineering, we had a special task force. We devoted a great deal of time in that group finding minority candidates who did not send in resumes on their own. As it turns out, our first choice was a minority who had just sent in a resume in response to a magazine ad, and the special task force never had anything to do with it. That says to me that this whole team was responsible enough not to allow prejudice to interfere. Nevertheless, until all people are that responsible, things like quotas and special minority task forces are necessary to enforce equality.

Soapbox over. And from that meandering style comes the true spurt of creativity that took off and never looked back. You would think that a mind like mine could easily create text with no apparent rhythm or path, but it is actually quite difficult.

A Night of Creativity

Grumble, slobber, spin
Another record set
Bump spike the head
Is at the back of the ship
Carries us to Paradise
Is a 15 hour flight from here
we are, in cage with rage
fill the creative being
still no more, spinning wildly
the devil of Tasmania flies free
Shackles, sputter, stumble
Climbing, growing until all
the world is at its feet. Happy to be
at its feet.
Creative free, on warpath
Tearing structure
World is happy

Never knew how good it was.
Save it, remember it, repeat it,
Write it down. Store it. Catch it.
Take its glory and box it up
Where all can see it at will.
Bound it. Tie it. Lock it tight.
Don't let it out of guarded sight.
A briefly glorious, fearful night.

That poem is fun for me to read, as well. A lot of times, I look at a poem I wrote and say "I should have done this," or "I should have done that." But in the previous poem, I'm not sure what I did, so I can't critique it, I can only enjoy it.

Kind of like you. I just seemed to happen upon you, and you turned out just right. Not that making life decisions is always easy (i.e. moving to New Jersey), but, as Albert Camus might tell us, it's life's challenges that make each day worth living and the successes so sweet. Although he'd say it without such jubilance.

And challenges are often a major theme in some of these poems. The whole idea of us being so far apart is, of course, a challenge of monumental proportions, but the rewards will be accordingly sized. The abstention from intimacy until after the wedding is, of course, another. But, again, the rewards look promising.

Being in this sort of relationship, though, we are forced to take a cleidoic view of the situation. We see the pain of being apart, the devotion to the telephone and to Delta and Continental Airlines. When we step outside of our shells, we see what we have as the rest of the world sees it, and it is quite beautiful. Ours is a storybook romance: separated by Pennsylvania, but with such a strong love that we can not be kept apart. Then, on our wedding day, we come together to start our lives together, thus completing the happy ending to the courting.

And in that light, the next poem was written from the perspective of the people of Pittsburgh, who, for one brief weekend, had the opportunity to entertain the love of the century (ours). This poem was written on the outside of the shell, by the people who were able to witness this great love (from the piano players at the pub to the late-nighters at the burger place).

The Night Love Came Through Town

Slowly, the air begins to fill with the tingle of anticipation.

The stars align for presentation to the crowd below.

Full force the voices proclaim arrival,

For the lovers arrive in Pittsburgh tonight.

Streets are lined with garments to soften the ride,

Possibly signifying the ritual about to take place,

Or out of respect for the princess's new tires.

This gala event is celebrated by all.

Quietly, the town follows and gazes

Hoping to catch a glimpse of the couple's pleasure.

Happy the room bears wine, plums, and grapes,

Somewhat distraught when he closes the drapes.

Silent, again, the visit draws to a close,

Knowing they had a hand in the eternal happiness.

Yet, still, butterflies stir when they think of the love

That visited Pittsburgh one fine summer's day.

The whole perfect romance discussion gets kind of mushy if I try to elaborate on it. An earlier version of this text did just that, but it didn't read back all that well. Suffice it to say that just about everything we do, when I step back and look at it as an outsider, reminds me of the perfect romance.

And I hope this book has a similar effect. On us, that is, not necessarily on other people. You don't even have to tell anyone about this if you prefer not to, but I hope, if nothing else, it serves as a symbol of how much I love you, and how much thought I put into our relationship. And if you like the poems too, that's all for the better.

One thing your father told me while we were eating breakfast the morning of the proposal was that you were always his little princess. It is from that conversation that the princess analogy appears throughout this text. You are well-schooled in the ways of charm, but, for a princess, you have a real ability to be down to earth and just plain fun. Basketball, for example, is not normally a princess sport.

I don't know if that makes me Prince Charming or not. Perhaps your knight in shining armor. You can call me Lancelot.

I don't know how well I fit into the role of Prince Charming, though. True, I plan on having a washboard stomach by the time of the wedding, but I don't know how suave and debonair I can be. I'll be whisking you away to a castle that is just a garden apartment in New Jersey, and I eat frozen pizzas in front of the TV instead of having elaborate receptions in the dining hall.

Not to mention the fact that I have this recurring urge to leap through the ceiling tiles to try out the world above the ordinary world.

Maybe

Tomorrow . . .

Spending time in rafters, see
Wondering will they notice me?
I realize I'm just a ghoul
Who's out of work and out of school.
I'm up above and out of sight
With the real world sending me an awful fright.

Never caught
Never sought
Just a refugee perched and distraught.

Nerves on end
But tomorrow's a big day
Waiting for people to say so dismayed
"Where is he?
And what can we do?"

Yes, tomorrow the meaning and glory will come

When work without me just can't be done.

Never caught

Never sought

Just a refugee perched and distraught.

Don't worry, by typing this out, I'm realizing that spending time in the rafters is not an exciting adventure, so you won't ever have to come coax me down or anything like that. Although, it could be a good publicity stunt to get some of these poems published. It can't hurt to have a little extra help.

I also realize my limitations as a scientist. After reading through the first few pages, I can realize where some of my thoughts on the universe were inaccurate. No sense in trying to go back and see where I goofed, I either deleted or edited them. It's bound to be correct now.

And even the role of Prince Charming has flaws, considering the only events I ever won in a horse show (an important past-time of princes) were the costume category and the non-winners category! I do, however, have some royal qualities: I like good beer, for example. I'm sure that's something I have in common with royalty. I wouldn't mind ruling the world, either. In fact, I think I'd do a pretty good job of it.

Anyway, this whole princess analogy was brought up a couple of pages ago, and you may be wondering which poem really used this idea to its fullest extent. That's were this next poem comes in, where you are Princess, which makes your parents King and Queen.

I raise up the need for the son-in-law to be approved by the bride's parents. Specifically, the age-old need to be accepted by the father. In the poem lies the ping-pong game, as well as the golf game, both at Lake Cumberland. But neither of these served to earn respect like guiding the boat and finding Wolf Creek Dam and my island.

My Turf

Slowly turn away, a glare of stone
Another should have never thrown.
Not a mesh, the king and I
As Princess looks with dashing eyes.

Another stroke and turn to see
Still one more miss 'tween King and me.
And wondering when the mix will be
I cast my gaze to shrunken sea.

This is where the prince was raised
through dark of night, or morning haze.
And I can guide us straight away
To sights and shore where Princess plays.

And King's respect I now do gain
And Queen is happy if my name
Is shared with Princess, who remains
My inspiration, and my aim.

For now I know there is no fear
To sit with King and share a beer
And he will drink & chat along
And graciously lose the next ping pong.

Now, of course, I will never be able to convince you that I did not feel a great pressure to be accepted by your family. They were all very receptive of the idea of having a new son-in-law around the house. But it is nice to actually earn respect of the parents, even if in such a trivial way as driving a boat around a lake.

Of course, driving through Hell (a blizzard-ridden Pennsylvania) that Christmas Eve morning to meet your Dad for breakfast to ask for your hand was supposed to serve as the respect earning move. Unfortunately, when I started to hallucinate as we drank coffee and screamed "BIG SEMI-TRUCK, WE'RE ALL GOING TO DIE!" and hid under the table, I kind of blew the opportunity.

OK, maybe I only had a severe case of the nervous shakes, and we'll never know if I was nervous about proposing or nervous from my 14-hour near death experience. Either way, I do remember him saying "I guess I can't stop you!" That was not the general sentiment, he was actually happy to see his princess getting married, but the words struck me in a funny way.

And now, as you read this, his princess is married. Hopefully, I took an airplane this time, and never saw Pennsylvania. It is strange to think of how your life will change after marriage. Some of the old habits will no longer happen. For example, I will probably never drink a lot of whiskey, head out to the bars, and wake up at Junior's apartment the next morning again. You probably won't ever take another road trip with the girls for a wild weekend in Richmond. Of course, you may actually do that, but it won't be the same as in college.

Is that just maturing? Or does our marriage (and the marriages of our friends) force these changes? Probably both. But it's not a bad thing. From now on, there will always be a shoulder there for you. And every time I (or you) want to do something special, there will be someone for whom it can be done.

(sappy, sappy, sappy)

This is what I think of when I think of standing at the alter, being asked if I am there of my own free will, without reservation. My answer will be an emphatic "YES." I want to build things for her. I want to work to make her happy. I also want to watch her create successes of her own. On my list of reasons to marry you is that you are very capable of doing just fine without me. You can excel in a career, you can decorate like mad, and you can be a terrific mother.

By the way, the list of reasons to not marry you is empty.

So what does all this mean? And what does it have to do with the next poem? Basically, I am saying that we are stepping up to a new plateau, ready to discard many of the mistakes in the way we lived up to this point. Don't get me wrong - we weren't doing horrible things. But the point is that as people grow up, they all look back on some things and just have to shake their heads. But that's all in the past.

Of course, we won't be perfect, that's hardly possible, but we will be great.

And that's what this poem is. A beautiful metaphor of me overcoming the wrongdoings in the past, and boldly stepping up to the challenge and excitement of the future.

New Order

Beelzebub drew closer still
To perch upon my window sill.
The night about was ever still
As my eyes fell upon the swill.

He spoke behind his grating smile,
"I've treasured this one for a while,
For someone blessed e'er since a child
Is so much pleasure once turned vile."

And I sat quietly on the bed,
Not a word to please him said.
I fixed my gaze into his head,
Into the evil on which he fed.

He took my strength, my looks, my health,
He took my goods, and all my wealth,
He beat me down until he felt
"There's nothing left. He can't be helped."

And then he stopped, the king of sin,
And slowly bore a sweaty grin.
He turned to leave, go try again,
But stopped, amazed - I summoned him!

He turned to see my fragile smile,
"I've known you'd fail for quite a while.
For I've been blessed e'er since a child,
And I can not be turned to vile.

"Your little victories, so you may say,
As I may stumble day by day,
Can't win my soul, it's not that way.
I've been forgiven, I'm here to stay.

"There's something deep inside me still,
And you can't know it, never will.
My love for her is with me 'til
The end of time, and longer still.

"You took my strength, and all of these,
But they can go with passing breeze.
The thing that robbed your victory
Is the love I have for her, you see."

I rose, and towered over him,
And watched it fade, his seedy grin.
I shooed him off, and as he went,
I closed the window to his sin.

Quoth the raven...

But now to move on. You recently mentioned that you may want to write a book. I was aching to mention this one, but had to settle for simply stating that I may want to write a book on computer programming. I am trying not to neglect our time, but to also make this a book worth reading.

I can now relate to what you would be experiencing, should you decide to write a book. Yours sounded like an interesting premise, and I'm looking forward to negotiating the movie rights.

Meanwhile, I've noticed that this is one of those points where the line between a book and a really long letter becomes blurred. However, I feel that one quality of a good book is that it appears to be speaking directly to the reader. Kurt Vonnegut does this, and I'd like to think that I am doing the same. Of course, this is fairly easy to accomplish when you are writing to an audience of one. With all that in mind, I will refrain from editing the letter-like parts.

Of course, all this leads to that random thought pattern that my letters have. I guess that's OK, but it does cause that sporadic shift from what was essentially a love poem to poems about living in the ceilings at work. And that's exactly what this next one is about. I'm not sure why this ceiling-dweller has become such a recurring character. Think of it more as a metaphor about hiding from society and reality, not so much as a guy who wants to live in the ceiling.

Again, the hopes for a dramatic conclusion are dashed, and reality starts to nip at my ankles, like the angry dog that bit my Mom that day...

The Hunter

Slowly stirred from dreamlike state
They start to funnel in.
I gently move to hear and see
From passages found quite easily
Here in the land of me.

Animal-like, they gather 'round watering holes,
return to the lairs
Through the labyrinth-like halls.

This is not unlike hunting deer.
They don't look up; they know no fear.
From this wire and steel tree stand
I am omnipotent, the mighty hand.

But who is hunter, and who is prey?
Should not the hunter possess free will?
Delineation is not quite clear.

Again, I must come to the conclusion that the only worthwhile part of jumping into the ceiling area for all eternity is the actual jump itself. It hardly seems worth it, so I guess I'll go ahead and stay down here.

Just to give you a perspective on the time this is being written, I recently found that my computer's sound card broke, and I erased all the files that were recorded there. Thus is the life of an idiot, I guess. Also recently, you chose the "leaf trimmed" wedding cake this week, and the first University of Kentucky basketball practice is two nights away.

And, of course, that holds tremendous significance. However, I think our stories are beginning to diverge. I visualize us sitting around, me 94 years old, you much older, of course, telling our great-grandchildren about our first date...

"He said there were going to be about 50 friends there," you'll say. "My entire family was invited, and I could bring a date. There was a bus that was supposed to take us down there and everything," as you confuse this story with the first Keeneland racetrack trip. "Then he shows up on my doorstep by himself, begging me to go down with him. Your Grandpa was such a pitiful sight, I had to go with him so he wouldn't feel friendless."

Of course, then I'll have to chime in "Her brains been gone for about 70 years now! The only time she's not telling outrageous stories is when her teeth are in the jar! She knew that night that she wanted to marry me, and she was already plotting how to go about getting a proposal."

Of course, I'll easily be able to back up my story: "One time, I took a date to Keeneland, and this old woman you call Grams showed up and tried to attack me! I've got the picture right here to prove it. She's all over me saying 'I want a ring! I want a ring!' while my date is taking pictures!"

Yep, sounds like fun, growing old together. Countless bubble baths, cuddling by the fireplace, beautiful views from South Street Seaport, and endless journeys into the night on a Bullet Train. Kind of makes me want to type out the next poem, a little commentary on my love for you, which consumes me. I only want to make you happy, and I want you to help me out when you think of ways I can improve. For now, just read...

Love

What love could ever compare
To the love I have for you.

If my love was a river
The Ohio would be but
A single, annoying drop in the night.

If my love was a diamond
The world would sparkle.

If my love was all sand
The Sahara would trickle
Between your toes.

If my love were a mountain
It's peak would pierce the sky.

But my love is for you
And it's wrapped in a box
Less than six feet high

But it's filled past the eyes
Which are drawn to your thighs
Night after night
When in bed we will lie.

I can write a lot of love poems, and there's a few more lined up in the pages to follow, but it never seems like there's enough of them. I guess I'll just have to show you how much I love you, but I'm sure that won't be a problem.

While I feel a thousand more love poems could be written before the wedding, every now and then an irrelevant poem enters my mind. This next poem came to me while I was at work. I was closely studying the details of the new wave of object-oriented design, when I noticed a couple of interesting characteristics of my fingernails.

Particularly interesting was the way it reacted to stress, which could easily be applied by the other fingers. This fascinated me to the point that I had to stop to write this poem.

In my defense (although it appears I have left myself defenseless to ridicule over my work ethic), it only took a minute or two to spit out this particular poem. One as frivolous as this is only limited by the speed at which I can write. The poem is already there, and I only have to record it.

So I recorded it. I will not be defensive anymore (on this page) about my work ethic. I would like to comment on people's tendency to get defensive when they are caught goofing off. If someone admits (or gets caught) writing a poem, making a grocery list, talking to their wife, picking their nose, or whatever, they instantly feel the need to legitimize themselves by explaining how they only take 45 minutes at lunch, they take no breaks, they get there early and leave late, etc. I'm guilty of such behavior, as is every person in business today.

I think it's ridiculous to think that you could work through an 8-hour day without having your mind focus on other things for certain periods of time. The greatest research facilities in the world are known for long coffee breaks and loads of bagels. We should not be ashamed to admit that we can not shut out the rest of our lives while we are sitting at work.

Of course, too much time spent unfocused can cause problems. One guy, who sat in the cubicle next to me for a while, had his daily routine mapped out so he never had to work. Everything from clipping his nails to a trip to the head, every day. By the way, the trip to the bathroom was a common way people wasted time at my previous job, which is why I'm gun-shy about taking care of that kind of business at work, but when you gotta go...

Well, I'd say all this meandering has served as a pretty good lead-in for the next poem, which concerns my thumbnail.

Thumbnail

Half moon creeps out
to take its place within view
Sharing spotlight with only
a few speckled clouds
who drift ever so slowly
'til they grow out of sight.

On the beaches, the surface
is dry, often cracked
and tarnished with scars
from battles one knows
Should have never been fought.

When pressured, the skies
turn a fiery red,
Contained, at the end,
by a hard band of white.

Intense colors reacting
'til the pressure is loosed
And all things return
To their own state of rest.

And after that moment of memorable creativity, I crashed. The poetry vault was emptied. I had been quite productive for some time, and had many poems piled up. So it was fine that I couldn't think of any more, because I needed the extra time to type in the poems and add the prose. But nevertheless, there was this ominous feeling that I would never create another poem.

So for some time, I wondered around like that, void of creativity. I could not figure it out. The only plausible explanation was that I had started my Iron Vest qigong training, and I felt drained. That certainly was true, but I didn't think it should rob me of poetry. But even so, this slump lasted into the beginning of my 100 days of dietary and daily routine restrictions.

But even so, and thankfully so, I still had many poems lying around that needed to be typed into the computer, and a lot of text to "coordinate". By the way, you were here in October, and started to go through stacks of papers on the floor, and I told you that if you were going to dig, I had built a couple of stacks in which you might be interested. You fell for it, but you had you hands on the folder that contained all the poems. That would have been a real bummer.   All those entered into the folder, some on Daytimer pages, loose sheets and scraps of paper, they all would have been discovered, and you wouldn't have a wedding gift. I hid the folder after that.

Another slip that hinted (ever so mildly) towards this gift was the idea of another book I thought of for my Mom. Once I mentioned it to you, not only was the "book" idea on the table, but then I had to come up with a reason to not do it for Christmas '93. This book in your hands was the original idea, and I didn't want to create the second one before I presented this one. Quite a predicament.

Also, I mentioned in a letter to you about my philosophy that Mom and Dad should always be capitalized. I wrote about it as if you should have already heard it, forgetting that I shared that idea in this book, not in a previous letter. But you didn't pick up on that (very subtle) leak, either.

Anyway, I've blown another smooth transition. Back to my creativity slump. I felt artless, rejected by my spirit, void of all creative thoughts. While wondering how I could ever get out of it, I walked into my Thursday night class early.   The view from the window reminded me of New Orleans, and it took me back to the trip my family took there when I was younger.   I felt a small bubble of energy welling up inside.   I knew I would be creative once again.

Inspiration

Long, drawn, heavy
sits the face at the bar
Cradled, nearly engulfed,
by the hand, its lone support.

It is all the exhausted body can do
to support heart in its proper place,
Drained of all lyrics
It resumes a purely mechanical role.

A glance out the window
presents a new view.
New Orleans-eske, with the
windows in bricks.

People just looking, buildings so plain,
The iron-wrought fence
And the church bells
Echoing through the streets.

The urge to sit in the sill
Consumes me, I'm there
'Til the cracking of plaster convinces me
that my moment is gone.

But even so, I now realize
Inspiration can never be far
When scenes like this
Come to help me move on.

And I can take you to that classroom and show you the crack in the plaster. I jumped up on the sill, heard the crack, and quickly jumped back down. So I never really got to enjoy the moment in the sill, but the view was still nice.

Shortly after that night, I was creative again, and I studied up on poetry styles. Then, I created, and this is the first mention I've made of it, the Sonnets. Yes, that's right, Sonnets. I didn't do very many, but I think you'll enjoy them. They were fun to write.

And after the Sonnets, there is one final poem, and then I drew the finish line. In a way, that is. Because just the other night, I thought of another poem, and I've decided to use it now, before the Sonnets. You'll just have to bear through this one before you can read the Sonnets.

But I really must put an end to new poems. I need to finish this book, print it all out, size the pages, and get it sewn and bound. It is now November, and it is time for this project to be wrapping up (get it, this gift needs to be wrapping up!).

That's right, November. Just 67 days until the wedding! I am quite excited about the whole thing, of course. Also, I am very much looking forward to our wedding night at the Cincinnatian. I guess you know that's the secret place, by now, but as I write this, our destination that evening is still my little secret.

I just thought that one day our kids might read this, and decided to delete a little of the "can't wait for the honeymoon" talk. If our kids our reading this while we're still around, don't come to me asking about what I deleted. I'm sure I'm too old to remember such thoughts. Just watch the Phil Donahue show and you'll get the idea - most of the shows are about sex.

Of course, if our kids read this after we bite it (well into our 120s, of course, you much older), then I must urge you not to dwell on the fact that your Dad couldn't write worth a lick, but instead to be proud that your Mom was such a wonderful person, and to be proud that your Dad was a great lover. Below is a space for you Mom to initial proving that the great lover comment is true, which she will know by the time she reads this (after the wedding).

initial here: _____

Of course, everyone knows that parents don't think about sex and all that, so it's kind of useless to continue this discussion. Somebody else obviously wrote it and inserted it at this point in the book to gross out the kids!

So kids, I'll go back to talking about Mom and discuss her amazing ability to make friends with anyone, without ever compromising her principles.

Honorable

Chameleon

Her boss, for example, skilled chameleon is he.

Quite adept, so he knows what to do.

He'll be green to your face, make you feel quite secure,

But behind your back he'll turn blue.

There are many like that, changing color on cue,

Doing well, that son of a gun.

But this kind of lizard is not worth his salt.

I would pull off his tail just for fun.

Other end of the spectrum, I point now to Her.

Quite a lousy chameleon, you'd say.

Pluck her up from her castle, place her down in the slums,

And her colors, they don't even change!

Yet, although it may seem disappointing at first,

An amazing thing now will occur.

This honorable chameleon fits in anywhere,

Without ever changing her color!

Of course, I realize I'm on risky ground, comparing you to a lizard, but the poem really is a compliment. It is kind of based on one of the things my uncle liked about you so much, that you can be so very proper if the situation calls for it, but you also blend in well with baseball and hot dogs.

Anyway, now that the extra poem is in, we can go ahead and move on to the Sonnets. If you'll remember, I gave you a book of Shakespearean Sonnets for Valentine's Day in our first year of dating. While I was writing this book, it became obvious that no book of poetry about love is complete without some Sonnets.

Ergo, I knew what had to be done. Notice how I slipped in the word "ergo" once again. That is my mark. No document of mine goes out without the word "ergo" in there somewhere. So if I ever have to send you a secret letter, and you're not sure if it's from me, look for an "ergo" to know if I am the author.

Say, for example, that I am kidnapped by Sea Dog, the famous pirate. He may try to send a fake letter from me that tells you to put my most prized possession in a sack and set it on the beach at midnight. Before you go and put yourself in a sack on the beach, check for an "ergo" to see if it's a trap.

Now that we have that important precaution under control, let's go back to the point where I knew what had to be done:

I had to go to the library to study up on Sonnets. There were originally Italian Sonnets, and then English Sonnets. So I wrote a couple of each. There was quite a variety of styles from which to choose, even from the Italian strain.

The rhyming structure I chose to follow, with rhyming lines denoted by matching letters, was this:

abbaabba cdecde

The final six lines could have varying structures, but this one caught my eye.

So the Italian Sonnets came first. They are supposedly easier as far as their content, which I will explain when we get to the English Sonnets. But, the Italian rhyme structure is more difficult to meet. You be the judge.

When All the World Does Fall at Beauty's Feet

When all the world does fall at Beauty's feet
And I alone am chosen to come forth
To stand there with her, dressed in white, and more,
My soul, my heart, must full of happy be
To know that beauty came to summon me.
But quickly, now, I must move 'cross the floor
For time does move, the months, they count just four,
But path through mires of men I cannot see.

Now Beauty shows me how to move her way

So I step up to reach the next plateau

And move in close to take her outstretched hand.

This quickly we approach our wedding day

As I cross over weaker men below

To stand by Her, and thus become a man.

And, of course, you are Beauty. And not just in that first Sonnet either. And while the poem indicates four months 'til the wedding, it's only two months away as I am writing this. Two months never sounded so short, but seemed so long.

Wait a minute, now the text is starting to sound like a poem. The whole structure is beginning to crumble. It's a good thing this book is nearing an end. I probably couldn't make it much longer without getting really confused.

For example, in the previous text section, I wasn't sure if I had discussed "ergo" or not, so I had to do a text search of the document to see if I had already discussed it. Incidentally, I also became fond of the word because my favorite professor, from our Control Theory class, used the word all the time when solving equations.

I mention that only because I want to be able to remember why I like the word once I become old and senile. And bald, of course. Actually, I never knew I had thinning hair until you told me. Never knew I had a prominent nose either, or that I went "doot-do-doot-do" every time I pay for parking. Ah, I've learned so much.

I did know that I wasn't very strong, and as I've mentioned to you in a letter (which I haven't actually written yet), I always wanted to be superior in some sort of physical way. Cycling was one chance, but I never really excelled at that. It would take too much time, and I've always had other interests, like a job. Breaking the arch of my foot didn't help, either.

One night after hearing a grand performance, a woman rushed up to famed violinist Fritz Kreisler and cried, "I'd give my life to play as beautifully as you do." Kreisler looked at the woman and replied, "I did."

I'm like that woman, who wants to know the feeling of greatness, but can't sacrifice my life to achieve it, because a successful marriage, family, and career security take priority. That is hopefully where my true greatness will lie.

But I can know the greatness of completing the Iron Vest Tai Chi (qigong, actually) training. I can accomplish the hundred days of torture required of me. And I will know that I am one of merely a handful of Americans who will ever complete the training. That means a lot to me personally. This satisfies my need to achieve something great in the physical arena. I thank you for understanding.

So this next Sonnet is about the sacrifices of the Iron Vest.

What Torturous Wounds a Hundred Days Hath Wrought

What torturous wounds a hundred days hath wrought

An ancient means to quench the souls desire

Or build it to a burning, raging fire

Where, through the rage, the warrior's eyes have sought

Release, to chase for coitus, finally caught.

And pushing hard to take the moment higher

To crest the peak, relax, now through the mire

But tell me, was the torture all for naught?

The answer: No. It must be clearly so.

For one who without food goes for a week

Will treasure every meal in life so full.

Like we, who'll toss so madly to and fro,

And at the peak, our breathless souls do meet,

A moment everlasting in my soul.

Today is day 55 of my hundred-day program, and I'm starting to feel alive once again. The days of complete exhaustion may now be coming to an end. My sweat barely smells anymore. It doesn't burn my eyes at all. I have developed that ball below my rib cage, and I've lost 2 and 1/2 inches from my waist, although I've only lost about 5 pounds. I eat 3 to 4 meals every day, when I used to only eat 2. I'm starving the rest of the time.

I write that down only to remind myself of some of the side effects of the training once I'm old and senile. Incidentally, the medicine still tastes like rotten garbage. When I'm into my workout and feel like slacking off, I think of you for extra energy to keep me going at maximum strength.

Yes, with 2 months and 2 days until the wedding, I have plenty of reasons to be excited these days. But it was not long ago that I felt like I was in a slump. I went to work, I went to school, but there was still a significant amount of time until our life began. While plans were being made, and we were looking forward to the wedding, it just wasn't as close as it is these days.

I was bored when I was up here. Sure, I could work on my secret robot monkey project, or plan for the honeymoon, but as soon as those brief tasks where over for the day, I'd sit in front of the TV and be bored. I don't like it when I spend too much time in front of the TV. It's a real waste of time.

But now I'm considering loaning my TV to Mark. That way I can go over there to watch University of Kentucky basketball games, which I think he'll be getting on some cable channel. I'm trying to watch less and less TV anyway, and sometimes don't watch it at all in a day.

By the way, Mark will only be without a TV for about a month. His current TV belongs to a roommate, and he's got a new one on order (some huge monster that costs lots of money).

Either way, let's make a conscious effort to not watch too much TV. That's why I don't get cable, but I'd be flexible on the topic, especially if UK games are involved. But now that Beavis and Butthead are being taken off the air, there's one less reason to watch cable.

Anyway, the general drudgery of day to day life without you is the topic of this next Sonnet. It is the first English Sonnet, and follows this rhyming scheme:

abab bcbc cdcd ee

The difficulty of the rhyme is relaxed when compared to the Italian Sonnet, but that is offset by the difficulty of the final two lines, which are to gather all the sentiment of the previous 12 lines into a statement as powerful as the ocean crashing on the shore.

The Clock Does Move, but Slowly Toward My Time

The clock does move, but slowly toward my time
When joy will sweep me up on silver wings
And whisk me off to take me where I'll find
My bride, with healthy thighs and shiny rings.

But how am I to think of all these things
When walls of chalk are all my eyes can find.
I can't escape, and Satan's chorus sings,
Their joy derived from finding me confined.

Yet, even so, her thought does perk my mind,
And, standing straight as I could ever be,
I rise above the devil's daily grind.
Anticipation comes to comfort me.

When all I do is laced with boredom's sting,
A thought of you can free my soul to sing.

And the thoughts of you are nearly constant these days. It's 59 days until the wedding, and I'm ready to clean out my closets. The only thing stopping me is the thought of a burglar happily finding all my stuff already packed in boxes. Nevertheless, I'll be starting soon.

I'm also starting to plan my packing for Australia. It shouldn't be too difficult, just take every pair of shorts I own!

And I think about having you here, and all the opportunities we have to enjoy ourselves. It's an exciting prospect. But, the fact remains, you're not here right now (heavy sigh).

Well, crap. In the span of 2 and 1/2 inches, I've managed to accomplish a major mood swing. Boy, writing a book is just an emotional roller coaster. And about writing a book, I now have a tremendous amount of respect for anyone who can remember what they wrote on page one by the time they reach this point. I keep going back to be sure I've covered all the main bases - mentioned that I love you, used the word "ergo," etc. Fortunately, this is easy reading. Also fortunately, I have spell check, because I've come across some major faux pauses!

Meanwhile, you have arranged your first job interview for your December trip up here. You'll be leaving your car up here. You'll be sending clothes up here. It's all happening. The wedding plans are being secured, this book is just about finished, the groomsmen are trying to find dates, our Moms are buying dresses, and we're shopping for each other's gifts.

Sometimes all this does make me feel emotionally shaky. You know, either happy for no other reason, or nervous, possibly irritable at times. People warned me that you would show these types of swings in emotion, but you've been covering it very well. Of course, you still have 59 days to prove me wrong, but I think you are doing a great job handling the pressures that come with planning a wedding.

My pressures come more from issues like your job, where we'll live, etc. Of course, you feel these, too. But when you call me to tell me something went wrong with a potential employer, I feel hurt, also. This next Sonnet, the last Sonnet, deals with the inner struggle to decide whether to move us to New Jersey or Kentucky. Even though the decision has been made, there's always second guessing going on in my mind.

"What Move Would Make Her Happy?" is My Thought

"What move would make her happy?" is my thought,
  To pluck her up and bring her out to me?
  This question in my mind is often fought
  And hard solutions don't come easily.

  Sometimes I think the answer's plain to see
  A job for her would wrap it all up tight.
  And other times New Jersey's not to be,
  My Old Kentucky Home floods vision's sight.

And thus, these thoughts do pull with all their might

　　'Til both, exhausted, fall upon the ground

　　And, briefly, then, my mind forgets the fight

　　'Til both revive and start another round.

I'll wrestle with this through our wedding day,

　　But, truth be told, we're happy either way.

That was the final Sonnet, and this is the final text section. It's a time to be mushy, and that is what I intend to do.

It's also a time to reflect, not just on the book, but on the entire period before our wedding. On the gifts we gave each other on the 8th of each month, exactly one month closer to our wedding day. That was as fun as could be.

Reflect on the hard decisions, but not for long. Remember the feeling of going out with your friends, having the comfort of knowing that I am beside you, even though I'm not physically there.

Reflect on my journey to make it there in time to have breakfast with your Dad, then to propose in the afternoon. Remember scores of mistletoe, and the surprise of finding a man on his knees with a ring in his hand.

Forget about that man putting the ring on your wrong hand.

Remember all the hard work put into the wedding, and the satisfaction once it was finished. And remember our love through the whole thing.

And please know that this book represents my portion of the work and planning before the wedding. I try to participate in as much of the planning as I can, but, obviously, you are doing a lot of work, and I'm coming in to say "That looks good." This was obvious almost instantly after we decided to get married.

But this book is something I've worked hard on. I've seen you work diligently on the wedding plans, and it makes me feel good to know that you want to work so hard for our marriage. This book is intended to make you feel good knowing that I have worked hard, too, to make our wedding day special. When you would call and ask me what I was doing, and I replied "Working on the computer," the real reply was "Working on this book."

So years from now, when we sit down to look at our wedding pictures and this book, we can know that they symbolize the strong commitment that we have for each other, the love we'll always share.

Now, just enjoy the final poem. If I'm close by, come give me a kiss afterwards. If not, just close your eyes for a moment and know I love you.

One Moment

Content in anonymity at center stage
Not an eye upon me falls.
So close to those I do not see
With black and whites lined up behind
The sounds, triumphant, ring about
While angels echo through the halls.

Across - another line has formed
A balance, this one colored bold
And center, dressed in robes, stands still
One dares not move, not even so
For all do softly wait for them
To have, and best of all, to hold.

An artful eye would quickly see
All lines are drawn unto the rear.
And as perfection moves in view
The Kodak firework display
Attempts to catch the beauty's glow
A lasting stroll, a walk so dear.

And soon her show comes to the front
And all the world breathes heavy sighs
We then begin a life and see
Our happiness through all our years
And fondly call back on the day
That tear of joy sat in our eyes.

www.ingramcontent.com/pod-product-compliance
Lightning Source LLC
Chambersburg PA
CBHW061742020426
42331CB00006B/1331